DATE DUE

NIGHT OF GHOSTS AND HERMITS

By Mary Stolz

Illustrated by Susan Gallagher

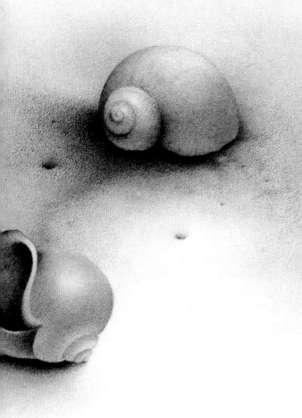

HARCOURT BRACE JOVANOVICH, PUBLISHERS

SAN DIEGO   NEW YORK   LONDON

NIGHT OF GHOSTS AND HERMITS

NOCTURNAL LIFE ON
THE SEASHORE

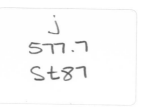

Text copyright © 1985 by Mary Stolz
Illustrations copyright © 1985 by Susan Gallagher

Library of Congress Cataloging in Publication Data
Stolz, Mary, 1920–
    Night of ghosts and hermits.
    Bibliography: p.
    Summary: Describes the night-time activities of the
hermit crab, horse conch, heron, loggerhead turtle, and
other animals that inhabit the seashore.
    1. Seashore biology—Juvenile literature.
2. Nocturnal animals—Juvenile literature. [1. Seashore
biology. 2. Nocturnal animals. 3. Marine animals.
4. Night] I. Gallagher, Susan, ill. II. Title.
QH95.7.S74   1985   591.909′46   84-15665
ISBN 0-15-257333-X

Designed by Dalia Hartman

Printed in the United States of America
First edition
A B C D E

To Gene, with love

—M. S.

To my mother

—S. G.

I would like to thank Jean Blackburn of Little Gasparilla, Florida, and Mary Parks of the Mote Marine Laboratory, Longboat Key, Florida, both experts on Florida marine life, who helped me to make this book factual.

—Mary Stolz

CONTENTS

THE CASTLE

Three brothers, Rafael, Chris, and Claudell, went down to the beach to build a castle. They took provisions—pails, paper cups, shovels, a sieve, a bag of Popsicle sticks, a small plastic pennant on a three-inch pole, a little empty bottle that a sample of mustard had come in, a thermos of lemonade, and some sandwiches.

Chris and Rafael worked all afternoon constructing towers and tunnels, battlements and balconies, a moat and a dungeon, and finally a ramp and a palisade of

Popsicle sticks. When they were finished, they stuck the little flag on the tallest tower and the mustard bottle on the lowest tower. The flag was to show that the owners of the castle were at home. The mustard bottle was a knight in shining armor, keeping watch.

Claudell stayed long enough to eat a peanut butter sandwich and drink some lemonade, and then wan-

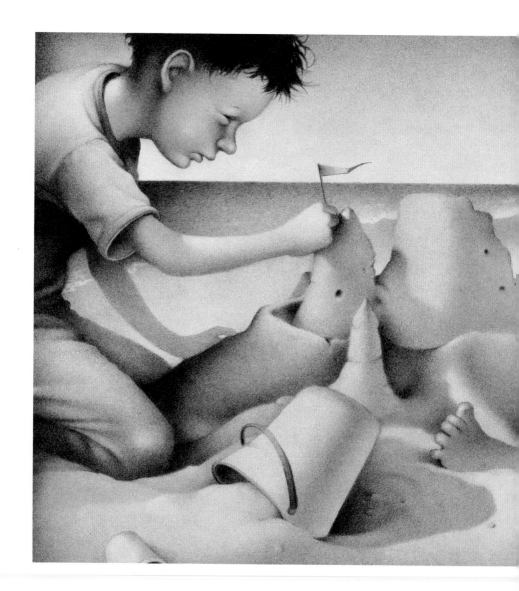

dered away to find, for his collection, shells that had been tossed on the beach—to find, stirring on the sand or in the shallow water, creatures that he could see and wonder about and look up in his books when he got back to his room.

His brothers were not surprised when he left them. Crabs and starfish, coquinas and conchs were more

interesting than castles to Claudell. When grown-ups asked the boys what they planned to be when they grew up, Rafael and Chris said something different every time. They were going to be astronauts, explorers, fire fighters, baseball players, tiger tamers, tennis players. Put another way, they didn't know.

Claudell knew just what he was going to be. "A marine biologist," he'd say. As far as he was concerned, that was that.

Still, when he returned with a few very good shells, some not so good, and six unbroken sand dollars, he admitted the castle was fine, and contributed several inferior shells to crenellate a tower.

Their father and mother came and took a picture, in case the castle washed away to sea. Then they all went home to dinner.

NIGHT LIFE

The world turned, the sun sank, the darkness came.

A ghost crab ran sideways up her long burrow in the sand and emerged in the middle of the castle yard. She stopped, chelae raised, and seemed to disappear. Surrounded by castle walls, she was pale and sand-colored, and she stayed quite still. Even a stalking night heron failed to see her.

When the heron had gone on, the ghost crab sidled tiptoe through the castle gate, over the Popsicle stick

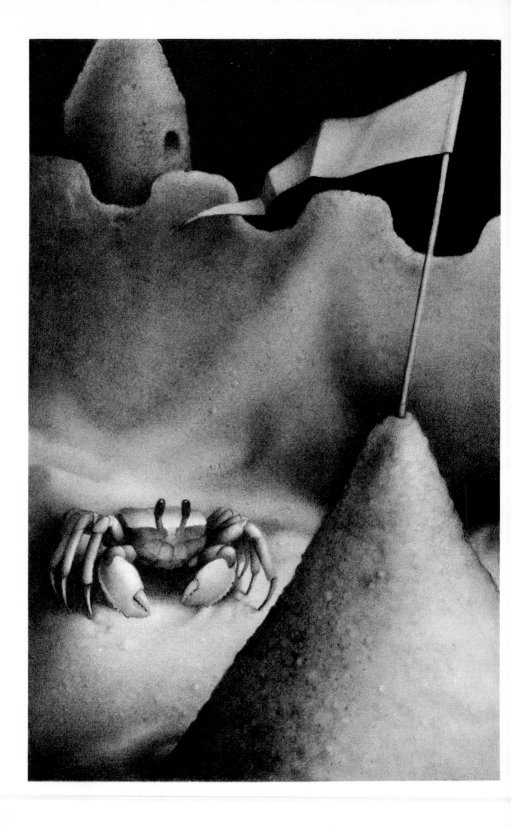

ramp, and down the beach to a mass of seaweed. There she began to feed on amphipods. She was always hungry.

The heron, too, was always hungry and, further along the beach, caught a ghost crab too far from either sea or burrow to escape.

If Rafael or Chris had come down to the beach now, they would have thought it deserted, unless they had chanced upon the night heron, or a great blue heron on patrol. Claudell would have known better.

He would have realized that life crowded, rustled, bustled, shoved, swam, spouted, hunted, was hunted, ate, was eaten.

Ranging the sea bottom, scouring the sand, were hosts of restless beings. Sea urchins and starfish and sand dollars mingled with pompano and cowfish and brittle stars and skates, with stingrays and lookdowns and calico scallops, with flounder and flame crabs and gobies and grunts.

Above them, sea slugs and jellyfish drifted by. Sardines and anchovies and tiny squid swerved and schooled in squadrons. Minnows swam for their lives. Larger fish fed on smaller fish, who fed on tiny fish, who fed on matter almost invisible.

In islands of floating seaweed—sargassum, turtle grass, manatee grass—shy creatures lived and lurked. Pipefish, sea horses, arrow crabs, and puffers. Filefish, transparent grass shrimp, moon jellyfish, cannonball jellyfish, sea cats, and sea robins. There were baby crabs of all sorts, small as nailheads—blue crabs, porcelain crabs, sally lightfoots, spider crabs, shame-faced crabs.

Too tiny yet to leave their seaweed shelter, one day when they were grown, they would venture out to join the other, larger foragers. Meanwhile they fed on plankton found in the seaweed, and sometimes on one another.

Capture and escape, hunger and the hunt, life and death ... the beach and the sea were in turmoil, and Claudell would have given much to be part of it, an observing part. He knew a great many important and interesting marine facts: that *chelae* are claws; that sand fleas, called beach-hoppers, are *amphipods*; that the Latin name for a frilled lettuce slug is *tridachia crispata*.

But, despite all he knew, he was only nine years old and was not allowed on the beach at night.

See page 48 for labeled line drawings of pages 16-18.

SYMBIOSIS

Just beneath the surface of the low-breaking waves, a large red hermit crab pranced on pointed legs. His house had once belonged to a channeled whelk, and was very handsome. Yet that was not the sum of his beauty. Atop the channeled whelk shell, he wore what looked like a rosy bonnet of ribbons. It was a cloak anemone. Riding like a passenger, it waved its pretty, stinging tentacles, repelling enemies from the hermit.

As they traveled, the hermit crab hunted. He snatched

at fry, at tiny crustaceans, at dead fish, and at other tempting morsels. As he tore at his supper, bits drifted up to the anemone, which in turn ate well. They got along together excellently.

Beings without words, they would never know that they were living in symbiosis. Even Claudell, the future marine biologist, didn't know that yet. Still, symbiosis it was—the living together of two creatures, unlike each other, but mutually helpful.

Symbiosis: a good word, and a good situation for the hermit crab and his rider.

WAR

A little battle, as fierce as a big battle, was taking place in the wet sand of the tidal area. A horse conch and a left-handed whelk were fighting to the death.

Nearby, a group of hermit crabs watched and waited. They were house-hunting. Two had been living in apple murex shells that they were outgrowing. One was in a moon shell that was too snug. The largest hermit was almost out of a tulip shell he'd inhabited much longer than was comfortable.

Of all the creatures on the beach and in the water, these hermit crabs were just about the only ones not looking for dinner.

They were too busy trying to find somewhere to live, and they awaited the outcome of the fierce, silent fight between the whelk and the conch.

When the winner ate the loser, a nice house would be available.

The hermit crabs waited for the battle to be over.

PHOSPHORESCENCE

And now, had the boys been on the beach and not in their beds, they would have seen a peculiarity, a marvelous and mysterious occurrence.

All at once, magically, billions of tiny green-blue lights winked and flashed on the surface of the water; they flowed along the outlines of swimming creatures and gleamed on the flat sand like mica in a sidewalk.

The light was phosphorescence, a heatless light, like the light from fireflies.

It seemed, for a while, to illuminate the ocean. A

fishing boat came close to shore and left a bright tossing wake. Wave after wave lifted and fell on the beach, like shining shelves toppling over. The moving fronds of the cloak anemone glittered as the phosphorescence surrounded it and its little chariot, the red hermit crab, with a brilliant bubble.

This marvel continued until the moon rose. Then, as the moon mounted the sky, its brighter light dimmed the sparkling particles below on the sand and the sea, and out went the lights, like microscopic matches, leaving beach and ocean to the moon.

HOUSE-HUNTING

The battle was over. The horse conch had defeated the left-handed whelk, had eaten it, and had gone his way.

The waiting hermits advanced on the empty shell.

By some strict crabby law, the largest hermit had first dibs. Quickly, he pushed out of his tulip shell, turned, and wriggled backward into the whelk shell. He pushed and shoved, and then darted out and back into his former home before it could be claimed by someone else.

Next, an apple murex dweller had a go at the whelk. He was too big for it. But the next hermit crab, when he'd left his apple murex and backed his way into the whelk, found it the very thing he'd been looking for. He squirmed into it comfortably, and then rose to his legs and walked briskly down the beach.

The smallest hermit crab, she in the moon shell, moved to the now-deserted apple murex to try it for size. Keeping the two shells close together, she experimented first with one and then the other, over and over for a long time. At length, she concluded that while the apple murex was a little too big, the moon shell she'd been living in was much too small.

Settling for the murex, she scuttled across the sand, still looking for the perfect fit.

BIRTH

The sea fell upon the shore, shattered into foam, drew back, and rode forward again. Each wave threw treasures on the sand: algae, broken sponges, sea worms, fish eggs, and plankton of all kinds.

The ghost crab danced along, nibbling, nibbling. Her stalked eyes rotated, watching for danger.

It was coming.

Step by cautious step, closer and closer, the night heron advanced. He was about to rush forward and spear the ghost crab, when from the corner of one swiveling eye, she saw him and she dived into a burrow. Running under the sand, she encountered another tunnel and raced along it, to emerge several yards up the beach, while the heron waited motionless at the wrong hole.

Another presence, huge and cumbersome, blotted out the moonlight and sent the ghost crab scrambling back into the burrow.

The giant loggerhead turtle was lumbering ashore to lay her eggs.

She had waited in the Gulf of Mexico for the night to be exactly right. She had waited for a low sea, a moonlit beach. Now she came, huge and heavy, in armor, dragging herself out of the water to begin her journey to a place above the waterline, where her eggs would be safe from the tide.

It was an awkward and ponderous process. Her great clawed flippers raked the sand, her body trenched it, her tail left a wavering trail as she plodded up the beach. Now and then she halted, turned her wrinkled head from side to side, and then resumed her slow march.

She encountered the sand castle and plowed through, toppling towerworks and turrets, smashing the Popsicle stick ramp and palisade to slivers, overturning and burying the at-home flag, sending the little mustard bottle spinning across the sand.

On she went, as unmindful as a hurricane of the damage she'd left behind.

At length, she halted at a low dune and began an excavation. Her flippers, like spades, threw sand to each side until she had dug deep enough to suit her purpose. In this safe hole, she laid her 103 round, rubbery eggs, and when she was finished there seemed to be a mound of 103 Ping-Pong balls.

With motherly patience, she piled sand back into the hole and covered and packed it until she was confident that her eggs would remain undiscovered until the night her babies would hatch.

Then, with unmotherly indifference, she turned and started back to sea. She had done her part. Now her children were on their risky own.

ROBBERS

The hermit crab did not care for her home in the apple murex. It was not a good fit. It was too loose and it slipped around as she moved up the beach; she was looking for new accommodations.

She passed in the moon-thrown shadow of the night heron, which was still on the watch for ghost crabs. She passed the ghost crab, which was still on the watch for herons. She fell into a rut left by the loggerhead turtle as she had returned to the ocean. It had filled with water and the hermit had to wade across and climb the other side, having difficulty all the while with her unsatisfactory house.

A few yards further on, she encountered an interesting object. Crowding close to it, she tapped its sides and its opening with her chelae, then whisked out of the murex and backed into this new possibility. After some experimental squirming, she decided she had truly found the perfect fit.

Leaving the apple murex for some larger hermit's use, she scuttled to the water's edge to feed at last. She was surely the only hermit crab on that beach—or any other—that lived in a mustard bottle. That she had taken it from the wreckage of someone's castle was no concern of hers. For hermit crabs, home is where they find it.

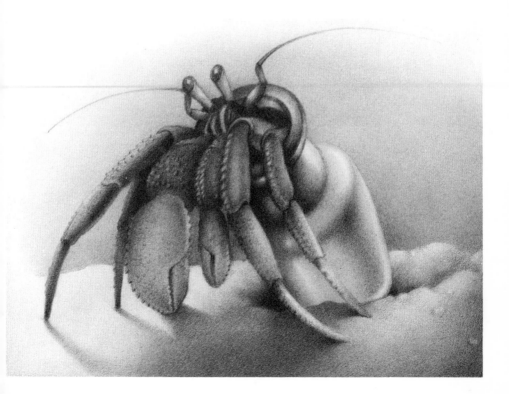

Meanwhile, the big red hermit in the water was having a problem, about which he could do nothing. A hermit even larger than himself had taken a fancy to his cloak anemone and was carefully detaching it from the red crab's channeled whelk shell. Gently, he squeezed it off with his claw, and then lifted it to the back of his own shell, that of a fighting conch. The anemone seemed

agreeable to the transfer and attached itself to the new shell as if it had never known another.

While this took place, the red hermit waited patiently, making no attempt to defend his anemone from the thief. After all, he'd swiped it from another crab and would presently be on the prowl to swipe another.

Crabby law: *Robbers keepers.*

SUN UP

The brothers were out of bed with the sun, and down at the beach to check on their castle.

"It's gone!" yelled Rafael.

"Tide must've washed it away," Chris said.

"No, it didn't," said Claudell. "It was knocked down by a sea turtle."

"How do you know that?" his brothers demanded.

"By the tracks. Look." He pointed at the disorder in the sand, at the two shoveled lanes, the deep depres-

sion between them, the snake-like line that marked the depression.

"She went up there to lay her eggs," he said, nodding toward the dune.

They walked over to look.

"See how she tried to smooth it all over, so no one would guess?" said Claudell. "Then she turned around and went back to sea. I tell you what—in about sixty days, we'll get Mom and Dad to start coming down here with us at night. Sixty days is about how long it takes turtle eggs to hatch. We'll keep a watch, and then protect them while they make their way to the sea. There are an awful lot of predators waiting for baby turtles to start for the sea."

"But won't the mother turtle come back to help them?" Rafael asked.

"Nope. She's finished with them. Lay them and leave them, that's turtles."

"Fine thing," said Chris. "Somebody might find her eggs and dig them up."

"She wouldn't care," said Claudell. "Next year she'll come back and lay another batch and forget them, too. She'll live to be about a hundred or so, and never give a darn about her kids."

"*Fine* thing," Chris said again. Then he said, "Let's build another castle. We got any Popsicle sticks left?"

"Enough for a ramp, I think," said Rafael. "We'll have to make the palisade out of just sand. And our knight in shining armor is gone, and the flag."

"Probably the turtle smashed them," Chris said.

"We got a couple more flags. And there's gotta be a little bottle of some sort we could use for the knight," said Rafael.

"But I liked the mustard bottle."

"We'll never see that again," said Claudell.

Still, if they'd looked in the long grass that trailed over the top of the dune, they would have seen it—walking away on pointed legs.

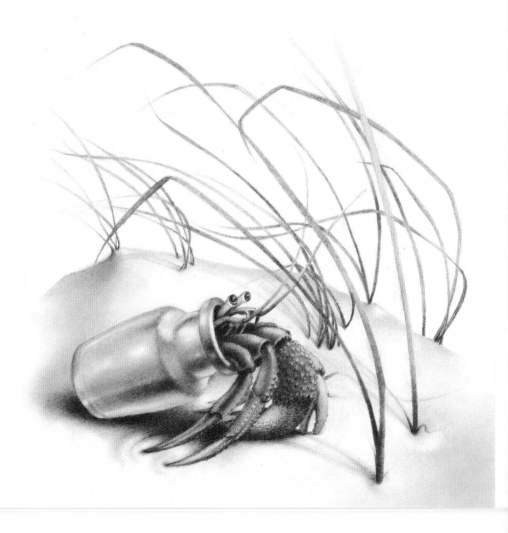

GLOSSARY

accommodation   a place to live

alga *pl* **algae**   a plant, such as seaweed, that lives in the water and is frequently red or brown in color

anemone   a brightly colored marine creature with a hollow, tube-like body, closed at one end and with a central mouth that is surrounded by stinging tentacles at the other end

burrow   a hole in the ground made by an animal, in which it may live

chela *pl* **chelae**   a claw or pincer on a crustacean such as a crab

crab   a type of crustacean that usually lives in the water

crenellate   to construct a barrier that is usually intended to protect soldiers

crustacean   a marine animal that has no spinal column but that does have a jointed body divided into segments and covered by a hard shell; a pair of appendages, such as claws, on each segment; and two pairs of antennae

excavation   the process of digging a hole

forager   one who searches for food

frond   a leaf

hermit crab   a crustacean that has a soft underside and lives in the vacated shells of other sea creatures

jellyfish   an invertebrate marine creature with an almost transparent body and stinging tentacles

loggerhead turtle   a very large sea turtle

marine biologist   a scientist who studies the plant and animal life of the sea

mica   a crystalline mineral that separates easily into thin layers

palisade   a fence of wood or other material that is driven into the ground, usually for defense purposes

pennant   a flag or banner

phosphorescence   heatless light caused by the absorption of energy and continuing after the energy source has been removed

plankton   tiny floating plant and animal life of the sea

predator   one that hunts, kills, or eats

seaweed   a plant that grows in the sea

starfish   a marine animal that has usually five arms situated around a central circular body

symbiosis   the living together of two unlike organisms in a mutually beneficial relationship

tentacle   a long, flexible, projecting part of an animal, usually located on the head or about the mouth

turret   a small tower

whelk   a large aquatic snail

BIBLIOGRAPHY

Aldrich, Bertha and Ethel Snyder. *Florida Sea Shells.* Boston and New York: Houghton-Mifflin Company, 1936.

Colin, Patrick I. *Caribbean Reef Invertebrates and Plants.* Neptune City, New Jersey: T.F.H. Publications, 1978.

Leonard, Jonathan Norton and the editors of Time-Life Books. *Atlantic Beaches,* The American Wilderness Series. New York: Time-Life Books, 1972.

Meinkoth, Norman A. *The Audubon Society Field Guide to North American Sea Creatures.* New York: Knopf, 1981.

The Ocean Realm, Special Publication Series: 13. The National Geographic Society Special Publications Division. Washington, D.C.: The National Geographic Society, 1978.

Rudloe, Jack. *The Erotic Ocean.* New York: World Publishing-Times Mirror, 1971.

_____. *The Living Dock at Panacea.* New York: Knopf, 1977.

Synopsis and Classification of Living Organisms, Vol. I, ed. Sybil P. Parker. New York: McGraw Hill, 1982.

Vilas, C. N. and N. R. Vilas. *Florida Marine Shells.* New York: Bobbs-Merrill Company, Inc., 1945 and 1952.

Voss, Gilbert L. *Seashore Life of Florida and the Caribbean.* Miami: E. A. Seemann Publishers, Inc., 1976.

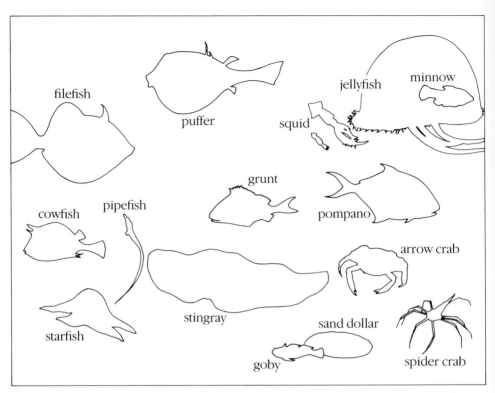

filefish

puffer

jellyfish

minnow

squid

grunt

pompano

cowfish

pipefish

arrow crab

stingray

sand dollar

starfish

goby

spider crab

Labeled line drawings of the sea life
appearing on pages 16-18

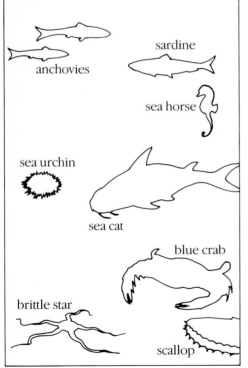

anchovies

sardine

sea horse

sea urchin

sea cat

blue crab

brittle star

scallop